Musical Instruments & Painted Moments

ADULT COLORING BOOK WITH POETRY AND SELF-DISCOVERY

Aventuras De Viaje

Copyright SF Nonfiction Books © 2024

All Rights Reserved

No part of this document may be reproduced without written consent from the author.

www.SFNonfictionBooks.com

INTRODUCTION

Welcome to the enchanting world where the melody of musical instruments converges with the realm of creativity, where the timeless allure of music meets the strokes of imagination. This is not merely a coloring book—it's a symphony, a reflection, and a celebration of the inspiring beauty of musical instruments and the painted moments they inspire.

Each page invites you to explore a realm filled with detailed illustrations of various musical instruments, from the elegant violin to the majestic grand piano, all awaiting your colors to bring them to life. These scenes, symbols of the world's rich musical heritage, call for your colors to reveal their stories. Coloring these moments offers not only a visual journey but also a profound connection with the harmonious wonders of music.

In the hustle of our daily lives, finding moments to pause and appreciate the wonders of music is invaluable. This book encourages you to slow down, immerse yourself in a world of intricate artistry and serene introspection, and reconnect with the timeless rhythms of creativity and melody. It's an opportunity to reignite your imagination and infuse it with the colors of harmony and self-discovery.

Set forth on this artistic journey, exploring the detailed realm of musical instruments and the calming act of coloring. Here, you're not just witnessing the beauty of music; you're engaging with its wonders, unleashing your creativity, and experiencing the tranquility of artistic mindfulness.

Discovering the Mosaic of Imagination

Dive deeper, and you'll find that this book has been meticulously crafted to enhance your personal journey:

- **Simple Activities:** Beyond just coloring, engage with activities designed to spark reflection and creativity. These gentle prompts will lead you to moments of introspection, serving as kindling for your inner fire.

- **Quotes:** Let the wisdom of personal development accompany you, illuminating your path as you add your own burst of color to the pages.

- **Positive Affirmations:** As you color, let these words of positivity uplift your spirit, molding your thoughts and inspiring a brighter perspective.

- **Poems and Haikus**: Delight in the poetic tales that complement the theme of this book, capturing life's varied rhythms and experiences. Each verse and every line serve as a muse for your artistic endeavors, enhancing your coloring journey with lyrical inspiration.

Embark on this coloring odyssey, immersing yourself in a world of diverse themes and the therapeutic embrace of art. Each page invites you on a unique journey, blending your creativity with the tranquility of coloring.

THANKS FOR YOUR PURCHASE

Get Your Next SF Nonfiction Book FREE!

Claim the book of your choice at:

www.SFNonfictionBooks.com/Free-Book

You will also be among the first to know of all the latest releases, discount offers, bonus content, and more.

Go to:

www.SFNonfictionBooks.com/Free-Book

Thanks again for your support.

Musical Gratitude:
Which song inspired you recently and why?

_____

_____

"Music is the divine way to tell beautiful, poetic things to the heart."

— *Pablo Casals*

I tune into the melody of my inner peace.

A melody blooms,
Strings of the heart softly plucked,
Harmony unfolds.

Harmonic Acts:
How did you bring harmony into someone's life?

_____

_____

"The music is not in the notes, but in the silence between."
— Wolfgang Amadeus Mozart

I resonate with the vibrations of joy and love.

In the silence deep,
Notes of joy and sorrow blend,
Life's song gently plays.

Melody Moments:
Describe a moment when music lifted your spirits.

_____

_____

"Without music, life would be a mistake."
— *Friedrich Nietzsche*

I am a masterpiece in the making,
full of potential and promise.

Whispers of the keys,
Echoes in a quiet room,
Music finds its way.

**Instrument of Kindness:
How did you help someone find their rhythm?**

_____

_____

"Music can change the world because it can change people."

— *Bono*

I embrace the music within me and let it shine.

Notes on the piano,
Dancing in the moonlight's glow,
Dreams take flight and soar.

Rhythmic Reflections:
How did you bring calm to a stressful situation?

_____

_____

"Music expresses that which cannot be put into words and that which cannot remain silent."
— *Victor Hugo*

I play the notes of my life with grace and confidence.

Woodwinds breathe in time,
Soft and sweet, they sing their tune,
Life's breath intertwined.

Lyrical Light:
Describe a time when you brightened someone's day.

_____

_____

"Where words fail, music speaks."
– *Hans Christian Andersen*

I find harmony in the diversity of my experiences.

Flute's gentle whisper,
Carries secrets to the stars,
Night's embrace is warm.

Musical Motivation:
What motivated you to be kind today?

_____

_____

"To play a wrong note is insignificant; to play without passion is inexcusable."

– Ludwig van Beethoven

I am the conductor of my own happiness and success.

Drums beat with a pulse,
Heartbeat of the earth and sky,
Rhythms weave our tales.

Song of Support:
Who did you support and how?

_____

_____

"Music is the shorthand of emotion."

— *Leo Tolstoy*

I celebrate the unique melody that is my life.

Ancient rhythms call,
Echoing through time and space,
Stories old and new.

Harmonic Happiness:
What brought you happiness in a challenging time?

_____

_____

"One good thing about music,
when it hits you, you feel no pain."

— *Bob Marley*

I create harmony in my relationships and surroundings.

Brass horns sound their cry,
Bold and bright, they pierce the air,
Strength in every note.

**Instrumental Inspiration:
Who inspired you with their actions?**

_____

_____

"A painter paints pictures on canvas. But musicians paint their pictures on silence."
— *Leopold Stokowski*

I embrace each moment as a note in the grand composition of my life.

Golden trumpet's call,
Brightens dawn with morning's song,
Hope in every breath.

Vibrations of Love:
How did you express love creatively?

_____

_____

"Music washes away from the soul the dust of everyday life."
— Berthold Auerbach

I listen to the symphony of my heart and follow its guidance.

Strings weave through the night,
Gentle touch and powerful,
Symphony of dreams.

Tune of Generosity:
Share a recent act of kindness you performed.

_____

_____

"The only truth is music."
— Jack Kerouac

I express my creativity with confidence and joy.

Violin's soft voice,
Serenades the quiet night,
Love in every bow.

Melody of Memories:
Recall a fond musical memory and its impact.

_____

_____

"Music in the soul can be heard by the universe."

– *Lao Tzu*

BEYOND THESE PAGES

A Deeper Dive into Art and Soul Awaits!

This book is but a chapter in a voyage where creativity meets depth.

Craving more? Explore the link below and weave deeper into the tapestry of art and emotion.

www.SFNonfictionBooks.com/Adult-Coloring-Books

A HEARTFELT THANK YOU

Dear colorist,

Thank you for choosing this book. If you enjoyed your journey, please leave a review where you purchased it. Your feedback helps more than you might think.

As the colors on these pages come to life, so does our shared journey in this artistic realm. I am deeply grateful for your trust and for allowing this book to be part of your self-care and personal journey.

By coloring these pages, you've not just created art but also woven moments of peace, reflection, and creativity into your life.

If you wish to explore more, there are other themes awaiting your artistic touch. Dive into new worlds and let your imagination flow.

From the deepest corner of my heart, thank you for bringing this book to life. Until our next artistic adventure together, cherish the colors of your journey and continue to shine.

Warmly,

Aventuras De Viaje

ABOUT THE AUTHOR

Aventuras has three passions: travel, writing, and learning new skills.

Combining these three things, Miss Viaje spends her time exploring the world and learning about anything and everything that interests her, from yoga, to music, to science, and more.

Aventuras takes what she discovers and shares it through her books.

www.SFNonfictionBooks.com

www.ingramcontent.com/pod-product-compliance
Lightning Source LLC
Chambersburg PA
CBHW081621100526
44590CB00021B/3543